Start With A Story...
by Ann Bryant

D0496320

Traditional Tales

Creating
Music, Movement & Drama
for Early Years

CHESTER MUSIC
PART OF THE MUSIC SALES GROUP
LONDON / NEW YORK / PARIS / SYDNEY / COPENHAGEN / BERLIN / MADRID / HONG KONG / TOKYO

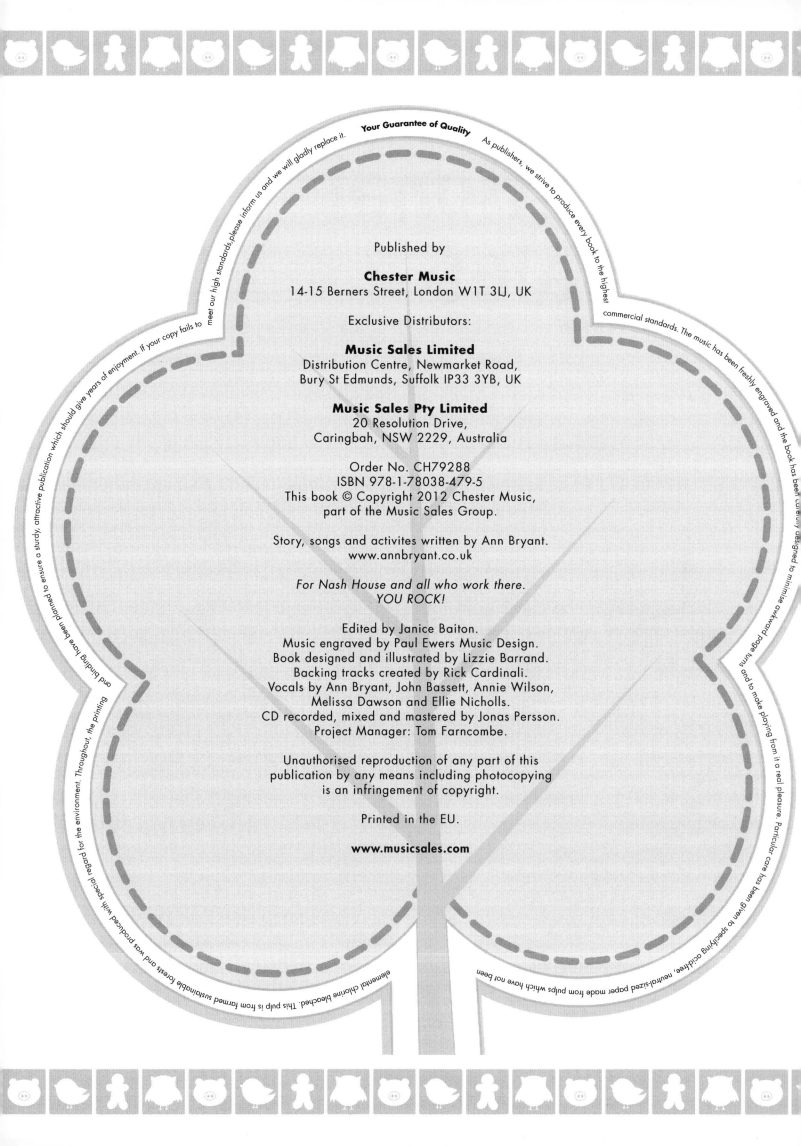

Published by

Chester Music
14-15 Berners Street, London W1T 3LJ, UK

Exclusive Distributors:

Music Sales Limited
Distribution Centre, Newmarket Road,
Bury St Edmunds, Suffolk IP33 3YB, UK

Music Sales Pty Limited
20 Resolution Drive,
Caringbah, NSW 2229, Australia

Order No. CH79288
ISBN 978-1-78038-479-5
This book © Copyright 2012 Chester Music,
part of the Music Sales Group.

Story, songs and activites written by Ann Bryant.
www.annbryant.co.uk

For Nash House and all who work there.
YOU ROCK!

Edited by Janice Baiton.
Music engraved by Paul Ewers Music Design.
Book designed and illustrated by Lizzie Barrand.
Backing tracks created by Rick Cardinali.
Vocals by Ann Bryant, John Bassett, Annie Wilson,
Melissa Dawson and Ellie Nicholls.
CD recorded, mixed and mastered by Jonas Persson.
Project Manager: Tom Farncombe.

Printed in the EU.

www.musicsales.com

Contents

About the author

Since graduating from the Royal College of Music and gaining a diploma in Dalcroze Eurhythmics, Ann Bryant has been teaching music, movement and drama. For over twenty years she has specialised in Early Years and Key Stage 1, writing many primary school music resources and leading workshops both in the UK and abroad. During this time Ann has also developed a highly successful career as a children's author, publishing over 110 books in these two distinct fields. Ann is a great believer in the integrated arts. She says, 'I love it when the two sides of my career overlay and overlap, which is why I have so enjoyed producing the four books in the *Start With A Story* series!'

'I used these books with my Nursery and love the way that alongside the fabulous music, drama and dance ideas, all aspects of the Early Years Foundation stage are covered.

The songs were hugely popular, catchy and easy to pick up and we have been introduced to a wide range of musical genres including traditional nursery rhymes, modern action rhymes, classical music, rap and jazz.

The stories in the books are written in a fun way that generates lots of discussion, and having the activities coming out of the story works brilliantly and gave us lots of ideas of our own, too!

But the best thing about the books is that you can use as much or as little as you like, since they are very easy to dip in and out of, so you can pick the bits that best suit you and your class at the time!'

Johanna Scanlon
Head of Nursery

Getting ready to sing – a handy tip
Pretend you are a balloon slowly fizzling as your air goes out. Make a long slow 's' sound as you let your air out and feel your whole upper body caving in. Now *very slowly* uncurl and straighten right up. Then you are ready to start singing.

Introduction

Each of the four books in the series has been specially written with a story as the starting point. The stories are utterly suitable for the Early Years age group, with familiar settings but also opportunities for learning. The books can be used in any order and can be dipped into or worked through. From the story emerge songs, poems and many other music and drama activities which all embrace and help promote the Early Years Foundation Stage curriculum requirements of:

- Personal, social and emotional development

- Communication, language and literacy

- Problem solving, reasoning and numeracy

- Knowledge and understanding of the world

- Physical development

- Creative development.

The story – **Mr Troll In Pixiewood Forest** – is presented twice in this book. First, we have the whole story. Then, we have each chapter again, alongside a song and a range of music, movement and/or drama activities.

The wonderful musical arrangements on the CD turn every song into a magical adventure. Look out for this logo  which shows where there is music for the activities. Even without the book, you are sure to relish the CD!

The activities are set out in chapters like the story itself. Some might act as springboards for other work. Many bear repetition and often benefit from it. The generic ideas which don't particularly relate to music/movement/drama appear in boxes with Mr Wolf to point them out. Feel free to develop the ideas as much or as little as you want. All you need is a space, a selection of percussion instruments and a CD player.

The characters in this story are derived from the following traditional tales, which you might like to familiarise the children with before embarking upon the story in this book:

The Three Billy Goats Gruff, The Three Little Pigs, Hansel and Gretel, Rumplestiltskin, The Gingerbread Man, Sleeping Beauty.

Mr Troll in Pixiewood Forest

Chapter 1
Mr Troll and the Three Little Pigs

In Fairy Tale land it was so quiet you could have heard a flower opening. The wind was still. Not a leaf fluttered. The only sound to be heard was slow sorrowful footsteps. It was Mr Troll. As he trudged he mumbled to himself, "I'm so ugly. Nobody likes me. Nobody likes me at all."

Then quite suddenly Mr Troll stopped in his tracks. He listened carefully, turning his head this way and that. Someone was talking. It sounded like a wolf!

"Little Pig, little pig, let me come in."

A little pig answered in a high, shaky voice. "No, no, by the hair on my chinny chin chin."

"Then I'll huff and I'll puff and I'll blow your house in!" came the wolf's deep voice.

"Oh no you will not!" shouted Mr Troll, nearly falling over his feet in his rush to help the poor little pig. "Stop that right now, you horrible wolf!"

The wolf took one look at Mr Troll and ran away.

"Oh thank you, Mr Troll!" said the little pig. "You saved me!"

"You're welcome!" said Mr Troll, and a lovely warm feeling spread out inside him. Then he looked at the little pig's house of straw. "Uh-oh! I think you need somewhere safer than that to live, Little Pig!"

"Yes, and so do my brothers!" answered the little pig. "We can't stay round here because of the wolf."

"Don't worry!" said Mr Troll. "I will help you all to find a new home."

So Mr Troll and the little pig collected the other two pigs and off went the happy little band. Trip trap, trippety trap.

Chapter 2
Hansel and Gretel

Presently Mr Troll and the three little pigs came to Pixiewood Forest.

There are lots of sounds in a forest. Leaves rustling. Birds singing. Branches creaking. Twigs snapping. Insects scuttling. Mice and squirrels and rabbits scurrying and scampering.

"Oh look!" cried Mr Troll. "That is the perfect place for us all to live!" He was pointing to a lovely cottage made entirely of sweets and chocolate, marshmallows and biscuits. "Yum Yum!"

"Cool!" said the first little pig.

"Fantastic!" the other two agreed.

"But what's that noise?" Mr Troll murmured. "I'm sure I heard someone crying out."

"It's coming from the back of the cottage," said the first little pig. "We'll go and see who it is."

So while the pigs went round the back, Mr Troll knocked on the front door. It was answered by an old lady dressed in black from head to toe, with a tall hat, a hooked nose and a very pointy chin.

Mr Troll thought she might be a witch but he still said, "Good morning, Madam," because he was very polite.

However, the old lady didn't even reply. She just took one look at Mr Troll, went very pale and slammed the door shut. "Oh dear," mumbled Mr Troll sadly. "Am I so ugly that I even frighten a witch?"

"Never mind that!" called the third little pig, from the side of the house. "We need your help 'round the back! Hurry!"

Mr Troll nearly fell over his tail he was rushing so fast. And straight away he saw what the problem was. There was a small boy and a small girl at the upstairs window. "Please help us!" cried the boy. "The nasty witch is keeping my sister and me prisoner! We can't escape!"

"Oh yes you can!" cried Mr Troll. "Jump out of the window. And don't worry, I'll catch you!"

The children leaped out of the window into Mr Troll's arms just before the wicked witch managed to grab them from behind.

"Get back here!" she called in her nasty screechy voice as she shook her fist out of the window.

"You are very wicked indeed," Mr Troll informed her angrily. He wagged his finger hard, which made the witch quake with fear and disappear back into the house.

"Oh thank you, Mr Troll," said the boy, who was called Hansel.

"Yes, thank you for saving us," added the girl, who was called Gretel. Then they both hugged Mr Troll tightly.

"You're welcome," said Mr Troll, wiping a tear of happiness from his ugly face. "Come and join us. We're looking for a nice new home!"

So off they all went. Trip trap, trippety trap.

Chapter 3
Rumplestiltskin

Soon Mr Troll, the three little pigs and Hansel and Gretel came to a glade in the forest where there were no trees at all.

"What's that funny noise?" asked the second little pig, sniffing the air with his snout.

"I think someone is crying," said Gretel.

"It's me," came a tiny voice.

After a great deal of searching amongst the trees, and calling out, "Where are you? Where are you?" a tiny little gnome came stumbling into the middle of the glade.

"Don't be afraid," said Hansel.

"What's your name?" asked Gretel.

"Rumplestiltskin. And I'm not afraid. I'm sad. You see, I've lost all my magic. I used to be able to spin straw into gold, but now I can only do ordinary spinning into mats and things."

"That's still very clever!" smiled Gretel.

"The trouble is, everyone used to like me when I was a magic gnome, but now they don't," he snivelled.

"Come with us. We like you," said Mr Troll.

"Oh thank you," whispered Rumplestiltskin. "That's very kind of you."

"You're welcome," said Mr Troll, patting the gnome's head, extremely gently.

So off they all went. Trip trap, trippety trap.

Chapter 4
Little Red Riding Hood

After a while Mr Troll, the three little pigs, Hansel and Gretel and Rumplestiltskin came to another cottage made of ordinary things like bricks and wood, and not a sweet or biscuit in sight. However, there were roses climbing the walls, which looked extremely pretty.

"This house would make a charming place to live," smiled Mr Troll as he knocked on the door.

"Do come in, my dear!" came a rather growly voice from inside the house. "I'm in bed!"

Immediately the three little pigs huddled close to each other and began to shiver and quiver. "It's another wolf!" whispered the first little pig. "I'm sure of it!"

"But he sounds kindly," said Gretel.

"No, he's tricking you!" said the second little pig.

Mr Troll was frowning. "Hmm! We'll see about that!" he said, striding into the house, the others tiptoeing timidly behind. Mr Troll could see straight away that the second little pig was right. It was a wolf. He was sitting up in bed, wearing a cream coloured dressing gown, a frilly nightcap and a big smile.

However, as soon as the wolf saw Mr Troll, his smile disappeared and he began to stutter. "Oh ... I w... w... was expecting my gr... gr... granddaughter, R... R... Red Riding Hood."

Mr Troll spoke in his sternest voice. "That is ridiculous! You haven't got a granddaughter, because you are not a granny. You are a wicked wolf!"

Immediately the wolf's teeth started to chatter and he slid down under the duvet until little more than his frightened eyes were showing. "I'm... I'm... sorry," he said.

"I should think so too!" said Mr Troll. "Now what have you done with Red Riding Hood's poor granny?"

"In... in... the cupboard," stammered the wolf.

So Mr Troll shooed the wolf out of the house, warning him never to return. Next he let Red Riding Hood's granny out of the cupboard and settled her in her rocking chair with a nice cup of tea. Then with a chirpy goodbye, he and his friends went on their way.

Trip trap, trippety trap.

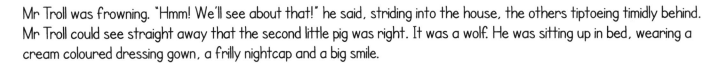

Chapter 5
The Gingerbread Man

"You're very brave, Mr Troll!" said the third little pig. "That's two wolves you've scared away."

Mr Troll's cheeks immediately turned pink with embarrassment. "Thank you," he said quietly.

A little further on there came the sudden clatter of racing footsteps. Someone was running very hard and ran right into Mr Troll's leg.

"Steady on!" Mr Troll said. "What's the hurry?"

A tiny gingerbread man was looking up at him fearfully. "Sorry, sorry, sorry! I didn't mean to bash into you. I'm running away from a man and a woman and a cow and a horse. I've got to keep running because they're all after me. They're going to eat me." And with that the gingerbread man rushed off again.

"It's all right," said Mr Troll. "We won't let them catch you."

But the gingerbread man didn't hear. He was already far away, crying, "Run, run as fast as you can. You can't catch me, I'm the gingerbread man!"

"Come on!" said Mr Troll to Hansel and Gretel, Rumplestiltskin and the three little pigs. "Let's try to catch up with him before the man and the woman and the cow and the horse do."

So off they all went. "Run, run, as fast as we can. We've got to catch up with the gingerbread man!" And it wasn't long before they did.

"It's all right," Mr Troll said to the gingerbread man. "You can stop running now!"

"No, no, I can't. They'll catch me and eat me!" replied the gingerbread man, puffing a bit.

"Look, hide inside this hollow tree trunk," said Mr Troll. The gingerbread man did as he was told and presently a man, a woman, a cow and a horse came along.

"Have you seen a gingerbread man?" they asked.

"Yes," said Mr Troll. "He went that way!" Mr Troll pointed towards a cottage where the three bears lived. He knew that for a fact because he'd seen a signpost. So off went the man, the woman, the cow and the horse.

"Oh thank you, Mr Troll. You saved my life," said the gingerbread man when it was safe to come out of the tree trunk. Then he climbed on to Mr Troll's foot and gave him a kiss on his gnarled old leg.

"It was nothing!" said Mr Troll, blushing to the roots of his green hair. "Come and join us, we're looking for somewhere to live."

So off went the party, which was getting fairly big now. Trip trap, trippety trap.

Chapter 6
The Prince

Soon the party came upon the most enormous hedge you have ever seen. It was very thick, very tall and very, very tangly and thorny. A handsome prince was staring at it, shaking his head slowly.

"What's the problem?" Mr Troll asked the prince.

"The problem is that I'm determined to get through this thick hedge because behind it lies a palace. And inside the palace is a princess who has been asleep for a hundred years. I want to wake her with a kiss but how can I possibly get through this hedge? All the branches have spun and woven themselves together."

"This is a job for Rumplestiltskin," said Mr Troll. "Come on, Rumple," he said to the little gnome, "we know you're good at spinning and weaving, but can you undo weaving?"

Rumplestiltskin frowned. "I could try," he said, touching the hedge. And at that very moment something amazing happened. The branches magically started untwining themselves and the hedge opened up leaving a lovely wide pathway straight through to the palace. Rumplestiltskin beamed from ear to ear. "I think my magic might have come back!"

"Oh my! That is magnificent!" exclaimed Mr Troll. Then he turned to the prince. "Well, good luck waking up the princess!" And with that he started to walk off, followed by Rumplestiltskin, the three pigs, Hansel and Gretel and the gingerbread man.

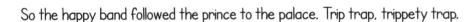

"You can't just go!" said the prince. "I could never have done this without you.
Come and meet the princess."

Mr Troll found himself blushing again as he beamed at the prince.
"Well, if you're sure…"

"Sure I'm sure!" said the prince.

So the happy band followed the prince to the palace. Trip trap, trippety trap.

Chapter 7
The Palace

In the gardens and the stables, in the kitchens and the great golden hall, in fact everywhere you looked were servants. But because they'd all fallen asleep right in the middle of doing something or other, they all looked like statues. It was an amazing sight.

The prince led the way up the grand staircase and everyone "oohed" and "aahed" at the sight of the beautiful princess who had been asleep for a hundred years.

"I do hope this works," said the prince.

And with those words he bent down and kissed the princess on the forehead. Instantly she woke up. Then a second later the whole palace was awake too and all the servants were moving about again just as though no time had passed. The princess was so happy to have found her prince at last and insisted that his new friends must live in the palace too. She was enchanted by Rumplestiltskin and said that now his magic had come back he could do magic for her, and if it went away again, not to worry, he could weave her a beautiful carpet. She thought the pigs would make lovely pets and could eat up all the leftover food from the kitchens. "So much better than throwing it away," declared the princess, clapping her hands delightedly. "In fact just as good as recycling!" Then she looked fondly at Hansel and Gretel. "It will be lovely to have some children around the palace," she told them with a smile, and added, "We'll need to get you some toys to play with but at least you've got the gingerbread man as a playmate. In fact any children who come to the palace can play with him too!"

Mr Troll was starting to feel a bit anxious. The princess wanted everyone else to stay but why would she want him? What possible use was an ugly old troll? He started to slip away hoping no one would notice. But he'd only taken a few steps when everyone cried out, "Come back Mr Troll!" Then the first little pig told the prince and princess how Mr Troll had saved all their lives and was the kindest person you could ever meet.

"Mr Troll, I was saving the most important person till last," said the princess, patting his arm. "I was going to ask you if you would be the palace's lucky mascot, but now I know how clever and generous you are, I would like you to also be our chief adviser, and live with us here at the palace for ever!"

Mr Troll could not believe his ears. "That really is too kind, your highness."

"Not at all, not at all," smiled the princess. "And now," she went on excitedly, let's go and have a great big party to celebrate! I'll lead the way."

So off they all went. Trip trap, trippety trap, clip clap, clippety clap, hip hap, hippety hap, hippety hap HOORAY!

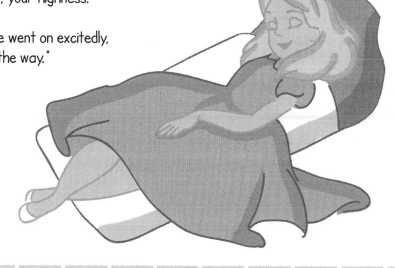

Chapter 1
Mr Troll and the Three Little Pigs

In Fairy Tale land it was so quiet you could have heard a flower opening. The wind was still. Not a leaf fluttered. The only sound to be heard was slow sorrowful footsteps. It was Mr Troll. As he trudged he mumbled to himself, "I'm so ugly. Nobody likes me. Nobody likes me at all."

Then quite suddenly Mr Troll stopped in his tracks. He listened carefully, turning his head this way and that. Someone was talking. It sounded like a wolf!

"Little Pig, little pig, let me come in."

A little pig answered in a high, shaky voice. "No, no, by the hair on my chinny chin chin."

"Then I'll huff and I'll puff and I'll blow your house in!" came the wolf's deep voice.

"Oh no you will not!" shouted Mr Troll, nearly falling over his feet in his rush to help the poor little pig. "Stop that right now, you horrible wolf!"

The wolf took one look at Mr Troll and ran away.

"Oh thank you, Mr Troll!" said the little pig. "You saved me!"

"You're welcome!" said Mr Troll, and a lovely warm feeling spread out inside him. Then he looked at the little pig's house of straw. "Uh-oh! I think you need somewhere safer than that to live, Little Pig!"

"Yes, and so do my brothers!" answered the little pig. "We can't stay round here because of the wolf."

"Don't worry!" said Mr Troll. "I will help you all to find a new home."

So Mr Troll and the little pig collected the other two pigs and off went the happy little band. Trip trap, trippety trap.

Thanks Mr Troll!

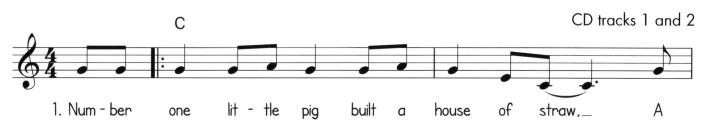

1. Num - ber one lit - tle pig built a house of straw,__ A

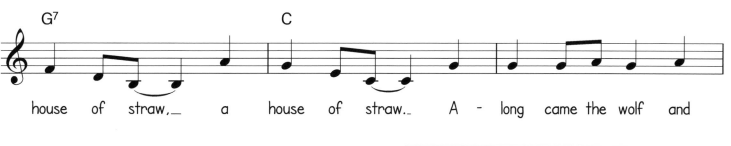

house of straw,__ a house of straw._ A - long came the wolf and

knocked at the door With a rat-a-tat, let me come in! 2. Just a chin!

2. Just a look at the troll and the wolf ran away,
   The wolf ran away, the wolf ran away.
   Oh thanks Mr. Troll, you saved the day,
   By the hair on my chinny chin chin!

Chapter 1 Activities

Let's Sing!

♦ Sing the song with the help of the CD (track 1), then with the accompaniment only (track 2).

Let's clap!

♦ Listen to the beat on the CD and clap along.

Let's play!

♦ First divide the children into two groups – e.g. wooden instruments, shakers. Each group takes a turn to play the beat (one group per verse).

♦ Swap around so everyone gets to play both types of instrument.

Sad and happy

♦ Talk about why Mr Troll was sad, and what made him happy later on in this chapter.

♦ What makes the children in your class sad/happy?

♦ Everyone trudge round the room sadly in time to the music on the CD (track 3). When the CD turns to happy skipping music, you change to skipping too.

♦ With instruments of your choice, all play to the beat of the trudging music on the CD and then change to the faster beat of the happy music.

Listen to the sound of silence

Discover silence like the silence in Fairy Tale land at the start of the story. Lie on your backs, shut your eyes, be as quiet as possible and listen to the inevitable noises of life! It is hardly ever truly silent.

Dramatise the traditional tale of The Three Little Pigs

Use CD track 4 to help you improvise the story.

1. Everyone imagine you are the first little pig. Go off and collect some big handfuls of straw. Drop them in a pile in a central place. The music allows for four trips to collect straw. You will hear the regular beat of the footsteps and then the 'dumping' of the straw!

2. At the change of music, start building. Notice how the music gradually goes higher, just like the house.

3. Speaking/role play. Half the class plays the wolf, half plays the little pig.

WOLF: *Little pig, little pig, let me come in.*

PIG: *No, by the hair on my chinny chin chin.*

WOLF: *Then I'll huff and I'll puff and I'll blow your house in.*

Play the track again for the second and third little pigs' house of sticks and bricks respectively.

Combining two rhythms

♟ Listen to the CD (track 5).
Half the class join in with the words:
Troll – troll – Mis - ter Troll …
The other half join in with the words:
Lit-tle pig   lit-tle pig …

Swap parts.

♟ Try both parts at the same time without the help of the CD.
Do plenty of repetitions until the rhythms are secure.
Clap the rhythm of the words as you say them.

♟ Now whisper the words while still clapping clearly.

♟ Divide the class into two halves. One half has instruments – wooden instruments for those saying the words 'Little pig, little pig', and something contrasting like shakers or little hand drums for those saying the words 'Troll, troll, Mister Troll'. The listening children will be able to appreciate the sound of the two rhythms going on together.
Swap over.

'If you're happy and you know it...'

You might like to sing the well-known traditional song 'If you're happy and you know it, clap your hands' and experiment with other actions such as 'stamp your feet', 'pat your knees', 'tap the floor', 'jump up high', 'skip around', 'play guitar', 'punch the air'.

Problem solving

What was the problem in this first chapter of *Mr Troll in Pixiewood Forest*? Who solved it? How?

Numeracy

How many people are there trip trapping along at this stage in the story? Choose a child to 'be' Mr Troll and three others to 'be' the three little pigs. Using these characters, show the sum

$$1 + 3 = 4.$$

Where did the story come from?

Look at the story of *The Three Billy Goats Gruff* as a separate entity and talk about the device of taking a bit of a story and putting it in another story. The tale of *Mr Troll in Pixiewood Forest* is the tale of what happened to the troll *after* the story of *The Three Billy Goats Gruff*. Mr Troll has become a nice character

Look at the story of *The Three Little Pigs* in the same way. In *Mr Troll in Pixiewood Forest* the story imagines what might have happened *instead* of what happened in the original version.

Chapter 2
Hansel and Gretel

Presently Mr Troll and the three little pigs came to Pixiewood Forest.

There are lots of sounds in a forest. Leaves rustling. Birds singing. Branches creaking. Twigs snapping. Insects scuttling. Mice and squirrels and rabbits scurrying and scampering.

"Oh look!" cried Mr Troll. "That is the perfect place for us all to live!" He was pointing to a lovely cottage made entirely of sweets and chocolate, marshmallows and biscuits. "Yum Yum!"

"Cool!" said the first little pig.

"Fantastic!" the other two agreed.

"But what's that noise?" Mr Troll murmured. "I'm sure I heard someone crying out."

"It's coming from the back of the cottage," said the first little pig. "We'll go and see who it is."

So while the pigs went round the back, Mr Troll knocked on the front door. It was answered by an old lady dressed in black from head to toe, with a tall hat, a hooked nose and a very pointy chin.

Mr Troll thought she might be a witch but he still said, "Good morning, Madam," because he was very polite.

However, the old lady didn't even reply. She just took one look at Mr Troll, went very pale and slammed the door shut. "Oh dear," mumbled Mr Troll sadly. "Am I so ugly that I even frighten a witch?"

"Never mind that!" called the third little pig, from the side of the house. "We need your help 'round the back! Hurry!"

Mr Troll nearly fell over his tail he was rushing so fast. And straight away he saw what the problem was. There was a small boy and a small girl at the upstairs window. "Please help us!" cried the boy. "The nasty witch is keeping my sister and me prisoner! We can't escape!"

"Oh yes you can!" cried Mr Troll. "Jump out of the window. And don't worry, I'll catch you!"

The children leaped out of the window into Mr Troll's arms just before the wicked witch managed to grab them from behind.

"Get back here!" she called in her nasty screechy voice as she shook her fist out of the window.

"You are very wicked indeed," Mr Troll informed her angrily. He wagged his finger hard, which made the witch quake with fear and disappear back into the house.

"Oh thank you, Mr Troll," said the boy, who was called Hansel.

"Yes, thank you for saving us," added the girl, who was called Gretel. Then they both hugged Mr Troll tightly.

"You're welcome," said Mr Troll, wiping a tear of happiness from his ugly face. "Come and join us. We're looking for a nice new home!"

So off they all went. Trip trap, trippety trap.

The Troll Went Rushing And Racing

CD track 6

1. The troll went rush-ing and rac - ing, The troll went rush-ing and rac - ing, The

troll went rush-ing and rac - ing To hear what he could hear.____ And

all that he could hear,____ And all that he could hear Was the

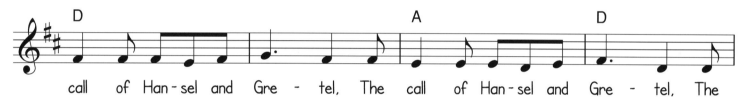

call of Han - sel and Gre - tel, The call of Han - sel and Gre - tel, The

call of Han - sel and Gre - tel Was all that he could hear.____

2. TWO PRE-CHOSEN CHILDREN
REPRESENTING HANSEL AND GRETEL:
The troll went rushing and racing (x3)
To hear what he could hear.

ALL:
And all that he could hear (x2)

TEACHER:
Was Rebecca, Tommy and Rohan...

ALL JOIN IN:
Rebecca, Tommy and Rohan (x2)
Was all that he could hear.

3. REBECCA, TOMMY AND ROHAN:
The troll went rushing and racing (x3)
To hear what he could hear.

ALL:
And all that he could hear (x2)

TEACHER:
Was Henry and Tobias...

ALL JOIN IN:
Henry and Tobias (x2)
Was all that he could hear.

HENRY AND TOBIAS:
The troll went rushing and racing...etc.

Chapter 2 Activities

Let's Sing!

👤 Use the CD track 6 as a demo track to learn how to sing this song, then sing it unaccompanied. It's much more straightforward than it looks on paper, and is great fun to sing once you get in the swing of it! It gives the opportunity for two or three children to sing alone while the others listen.

👤 Remember when singing unaccompanied it's important to find a good place in your vocal range for the starting note. This varies from song to song and comes with practice. Small children have a small vocal range, so try to tune into their voices. Ask a child who you perceive to be quite tuneful to sing any song of his/her choice, e.g. 'The Wheels On The Bus', and then you sing it at that same pitch. It might feel higher than you want to sing instinctively.

👤 Sit the children in a banana shape so they can all see you easily. The song can roll on for as long as you want. The children need to be listening carefully for their name. Fit the names into the rhythm of the music as best you can by adjusting the pattern of the words slightly if necessary, e.g. 'Was the call of Sarah and Rani' or 'Was Ayesha and Jonno together'. If you would like a solo, you might sing something like 'Was Natasha all on her own', 'Was Jake, and he sang a solo' OR 'Was Tia all by herself'. Experiment!

Numeracy
Play a game where you play a drum:
One tap = get into a space of your own
Two taps = get into pairs like Hansel and Gretel.
Three taps = get into threes like the three little pigs
Four taps = get into fours like the three little pigs and Mr Troll
Five taps = get into fives like the three little pigs and Hansel and Gretel
Six taps = get into sixes like the three little pigs, Hansel, Gretel and Mr Troll.
(The last two or three of these will perhaps be too demanding!)

Numeracy
How many people have we got in the story now? Again, the children should represent the characters in the story. We had four before and now we are adding Hansel and Gretel to make six.

Where did the story come from?
Look at the traditional tale of *Hansel and Gretel*. Now think about Pixiewood Forest in 'our' story. At what point does 'our' story drop into the original story? Talk about how we don't have the father and stepmother in 'our' story and we don't see Hansel and Gretel walking in the forest. We only find them calling out for help in the cottage of sweets. After that how is the story different? There are no trolls or pigs in the original tale and they don't get rescued.

Let's play!

🪆 Try adapting the concept (small group and whole class) of the 'Let's Sing!' activity from voices to instruments.

🪆 Divide the children into five groups. Within each group, each child should have the same type of instrument, e.g. sandblocks, shakers, tambourines, jingle bells. If you don't have enough of the same instruments, work with half the class at a time. (Tell the watching and listening children it will be their turn next, but first they have to help you see who was paying attention and playing their instrument at exactly the right time.)

🪆 Don't attempt to have any rhythmic framework for this activity. It's simply an exercise in encouraging children to be alert, to look and to listen. Show the children what hand signal (your choice) you will make when you want them all to play together, and what signal for all to be silent (maybe a finger to the lips) and what signal to indicate that you want only one group to play (maybe simply point).

A poem –
The Animals Of The Forest
(track 7)

Ants and beetles scuttle all around
Can you hear that scuttle scuttle sound?
Scuttle scuttle scuttle, scuttle scuttle scuttle
Scuttle scuttle scuttle on the ground.

Lots of little mice scurry all around
Can you hear that scurry scurry sound?
Scurry scurry scurry, scurry scurry scurry
Scurry scurry scurry on the ground.

Squirrels and rabbits scamper all around
Can you hear that scamper scamper sound?
Scamper scamper scamper,
scamper scamper scamper
Scamper scamper scamper on the ground.

CD track 7 shows you how the words fit into the rhythm of the poem. During the first two lines of each verse, everyone go round the room with the tiniest, lightest jogging footsteps. Then stop and 'scrabble' fingers on the floor for the rest of the verse

Once the children know the words, try it without the CD.

Art and craft
There is a great deal of scope for art and craft work here, creating the 'delicious' cottage of sweets and chocolates, marshmallows and biscuits and liquorice allsorts. You might like to use sweet wrappers.

Role play
Make one corner of the room into an old-fashioned sweet shop.

Tasting sweets!
Try tasting different kinds of sweets from different countries. Make a bar chart to show who liked what.

Getting higher and lower

♣ Now for some faster action.
Bend down low and use your hands to be the
squirrels' strong front legs scrabbling up the tree.
Finish with your hands high above your head.
Then show the squirrel scrabbling back down again.
Don't race up and down! Keep it steady just moving
a few centimetres at a time.

♣ Now listen to the CD track 8.
Everyone needs to listen for whether the music is going up or
down. If it starts on a high note, stretch your hands high, ready
to go down the tree, if it starts on a low note, crouch down,
ready to go up. It might trick you and do two consecutive runs
in the same direction!

♣ If you have a xylophone, show the children how the larger
bars make lower sounds and the smaller bars make higher
sounds and ask them to watch and see whether you are
starting at the top or the bottom. Try the squirrel
scrabbling action as you play ascending
or descending notes.

♣ Then hide the xylophone from the children's view
and play either a high or a low starting note.
Can the children get into position to go up
or down according to whether they
think your starting note is
high or low?

Getting taller

♣ In a space of your own,
curl up into a ball then very
slowly grow into a tall tree.
You've only got two arms to
be the branches but each time
you grow, try to grow into a
different shape.

Chapter 3
Rumplestiltskin

Soon Mr Troll, the three little pigs and Hansel and Gretel came to a glade in the forest where there were no trees at all.

"What's that funny noise?" asked the second little pig, sniffing the air with his snout.

"I think someone is crying," said Gretel.

"It's me," came a tiny voice.

After a great deal of searching amongst the trees, and calling out, "Where are you? Where are you?" a tiny little gnome came stumbling into the middle of the glade.

"Don't be afraid," said Hansel.

"What's your name?" asked Gretel.

"Rumplestiltskin. And I'm not afraid. I'm sad. You see, I've lost all my magic. I used to be able to spin straw into gold, but now I can only do ordinary spinning into mats and things."

"That's still very clever!" smiled Gretel.

"The trouble is, everyone used to like me when I was a magic gnome, but now they don't," he snivelled.

"Come with us. We like you," said Mr Troll.

"Oh thank you," whispered Rumplestiltskin. "That's very kind of you."

"You're welcome," said Mr Troll, patting the gnome's head, extremely gently.

So off they all went. Trip trap, trippety trap.

Rumplestiltskin Lost His Magic

CD tracks 9 and 10

1. Rum - ple - stilt - skin   lost   his   ma - gic,   How   can   he   get   it

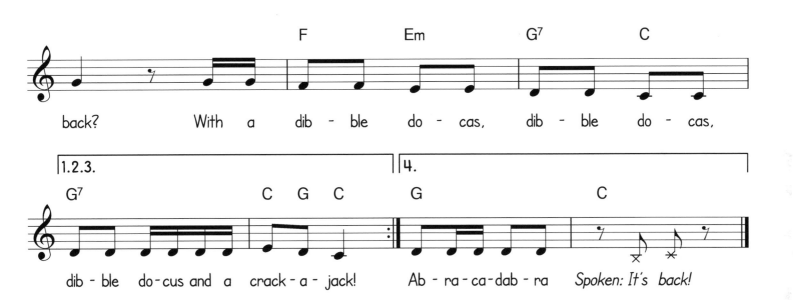

back?   With   a   dib - ble   do - cas,   dib - ble   do - cas,

dib - ble   do-cus and a   crack - a - jack!   Ab - ra - ca - dab - ra   *Spoken: It's back!*

2. Rumplestiltskin lost his magic,
   How can he get it back?
   With an izzy wizzy, izzy wizzy,
   Izzy wizzy and a crack-a-jack!

3. ...With a ba ba basha, ba ba basha,
   Ba ba basha and a crack-a-jack!

4. ...With an abracadabra, abracadabra,
   Abracadabra. It's back!

Let's Sing!

CD tracks 9 and 10

♣ As you sing the song, pretend to wave a magic wand on the 'magic spell' words each time.

♣ Make up your own magic spell words and sing them with the backing track.

Where did the story come from?
Look at the story of *Rumplestiltskin* as a separate entity. Is Rumplestiltskin unhappy in the traditional story? Does he seem anxious or worried? No. Yet, he is completely different in our story. Why is that? Is it because he has lost his magic?

Mixing the magic spells

♣ Pick any two sets of magic spell words. Divide the class into two and allocate one set of spell words to each group. Practise with the two groups separately. Tell the children to look at you and listen carefully because you are going to count to four (at a steady speed) so that everyone then starts saying their magic words at the same time. Now and in the future always call this the 'getting ready counting' and lay great emphasis on it. Try to count to a definite consistent beat at a speed at which the children will then repeatedly chant their spells.

♣ Next try chanting the two different spells at the same time. With practice you should be able to achieve perfect rhythmic coordination between the two groups.

Stepping at three speeds

♣ Mr Troll is tall. He takes long strides when he walks. The three little pigs are smaller so they take smaller steps. Rumplestiltskin is very tiny so he jogs along with teeny steps. Mr Troll's long steps mean that he walks at a slow pace, the pigs walk at a medium pace, and Rumplestiltskin at a quick pace.
Listen to CD track 11.
Can the children hear the three different paces? Do they notice the exact moment that the pace changes.

♣ Everyone walk/jog round the room matching your footsteps to the music on the CD.

♣ Organise the children into three groups, representing those three characters and their relative speeds of walking. Allocate a starting place for each group. This time when the music on the CD changes from one pace to another, the children must remember which characters they are supposed to be representing and only walk/jog round when it is 'their music'.

♣ On a given signal from you, the groups of children should move round ready to become the next character. Keep playing the track so everyone gets a turn at all the roles.

Clapping at three different speeds

♣ Using the CD, transfer those three stepping actions to clapping, so the three groups simply clap at their allocated speed rather than walking round.

Playing percussion at three different speeds

♣ Making sure that you have like-sounding instruments within each group, the children should play at their allocated speed on their percussion instruments. This might drown out the music on the CD, in which case, simply take turns without the CD.

♣ Now talk about the instruments you chose. Should Mr Troll's sound be heavier (louder) than the other two, or quieter? What about Rumplestiltskin's sound? Try again with appropriate instruments.

Low and high

👤 Listen to the voices of Mr Troll and Rumplestiltskin on the CD, track 12. Can you work out which is which? How can you tell? Describe the voices. The children might use words such as 'low', 'heavy', 'deep', 'booming', 'high', 'light', 'squeaky', 'tiny'.

👤 Seated in a circle, the children take turns to say the words 'Hello everyone'. They can choose to speak in a high voice like Rumplestiltskin or a low voice like Mr Troll, or their own voice, which will be pitched somewhere in the middle. After each child has spoken, the others must say which voice they thought it was. Children often find this tricky. It takes confidence!

Pass the cards

👤 You'll need to make three cards for the children: one each of a pig, a troll and a gnome.

👤 The children should sit in a circle. With any piece of music on a CD of your choice, pass the cards round the circle. When you stop the music, each child holding a card must look at it to see which voice type they must use then simply say the word 'Hello' in that voice type. For the pig they should use their own voice. Can the other children guess which character they were representing?

High, medium and low sounding instruments

Musical instruments often make higher and lower sounds according to their size. Listen to the short extracts on the CD track 13, of the violin (high), the cello (medium) and the double bass (low). Show the pictures of these three so children can see their comparative sizes and learn their names. Now play the music again and see if the children can say which instrument is playing just by listening?

Try that with the extracts on CD track 14 for the flute (high), the oboe (medium) and the bassoon (low). Can you find pictures of these instruments?

Talk about the extracts using any descriptive words, e.g. happy, sad, fast, slow, high, low, smooth, jumpy. etc.

High   Medium   Low

Violin

Cello

Double Bass

Chapter 4
Little Red Riding Hood

After a while Mr Troll, the three little pigs, Hansel and Gretel and Rumplestiltskin came to another cottage made of ordinary things like bricks and wood, and not a sweet or biscuit in sight. However, there were roses climbing the walls, which looked extremely pretty.

"This house would make a charming place to live," smiled Mr Troll as he knocked on the door.

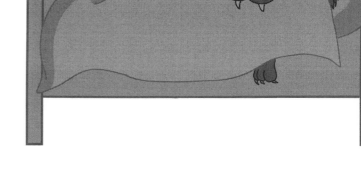

"Do come in, my dear!" came a rather growly voice from inside the house. "I'm in bed!"

Immediately the three little pigs huddled close to each other and began to shiver and quiver. "It's another wolf!" whispered the first little pig. "I'm sure of it!"

"But he sounds kindly," said Gretel.

"No, he's tricking you!" said the second little pig.

Mr Troll was frowning. "Hmm! We'll see about that!" he said, striding into the house, the others tiptoeing timidly behind. Mr Troll could see straight away that the second little pig was right. It was a wolf. He was sitting up in bed, wearing a cream coloured dressing gown, a frilly nightcap and a big smile.

However, as soon as the wolf saw Mr Troll, his smile disappeared and he began to stutter. "Oh ... I w... w... was expecting my gr... gr... granddaughter, R... R... Red Riding Hood."

Mr Troll spoke in his sternest voice. "That is ridiculous! You haven't got a granddaughter, because you are not a granny. You are a wicked wolf!"

Immediately the wolf's teeth started to chatter and he slid down under the duvet until little more than his frightened eyes were showing. "I'm... I'm... sorry," he said.

"I should think so too!" said Mr Troll. "Now what have you done with Red Riding Hood's poor granny?"

"In... in... the cupboard," stammered the wolf.

So Mr Troll shooed the wolf out of the house, warning him never to return. Next he let Red Riding Hood's granny out of the cupboard and settled her in her rocking chair with a nice cup of tea. Then with a chirpy goodbye, he and his friends went on their way.

Trip trap, trippety trap.

Strolling In The Wood

CD tracks 15 and 16

1. Here we go stroll - ing   in   the wood,   Stroll - ing with   Red   Rid - ing Hood.

Crunch - ing leaves,   crunch - ing leaves,   Come on   a   stroll in   the   wood.

2. Here we go strolling in the wood,
    Strolling with Red Riding Hood.
    Snapping twigs, snapping twigs,
    Come on a stroll in the wood.

3. ...Climbing trees, climbing trees...

4. ...Flying like birds, flying like birds...

5. ...Crawling like ants, crawling like ants...

Let's Sing!

CD tracks 15 and 16

🧍 Sit and sing the song with appropriate hand actions on the third line each time.

Let's move!

🧍 Listen to the song on the CD (track 15) whilst strolling round in time to the slow beat and changing to the relevant movement (using the whole body rather than just the hand) on the third line each time. Children find such slow walking quite tricky. If anyone is managing to keep to the beat, ask them to show the others, who should clap in time with that child's footsteps. Children should stand perfectly still on the last word ('wood') of each verse. There is no music between verses so they must think quickly what the next action is going to be. You could prepare the children during this music by saying what the next action is going to be. For 'crunching' do very small shuffling steps. For 'snapping twigs,' stamping steps. The others are obvious!

Let's play percussion!

🧍 Divide the children into five groups. Crunching = shakers, Snapping = woodblocks, Climbing = glocks, Flying = jingle bells, Crawling = guiros

🧍 Accompany CD track 15 as follows: All the children play on the beat during the first, second and fourth lines of each verse. (The children playing glocks can play on any bars of the glock). On the third line of each verse, only the relevant group plays. There is no need to stick to a beat for this third line. The idea here is to recognise the relevance of the chosen sounds to the words, and to be ready and alert as to when it is your turn to play and when *not to play*! For verse 3, 'climbing trees', the glocks should play from the bottom bar to the top one.

Where did the story come from?

Look at the traditional tale *Red Riding Hood* and discuss the similarities and differences with 'our' story. It is interesting to note that Red Riding Hood herself doesn't actually appear in 'our' story.

Numeracy

How many people have we got in the story now?

Let's chant!

👤 Explore the senses of hearing, seeing, tasting and smelling by chanting this well-known part of the original tale in two halves of the class.

RED RIDING HOOD: Oh Grandma, what big ears you've got!
WOLF: All the better to *hear* you with!

RED RIDING HOOD: Oh Grandma, what big eyes you've got!
WOLF: All the better to *see* you with!

nose = smell
teeth = eat you up!

Chopping Wood

👤 In a space of your own, try doing a chopping action to match the beat of the music on the CD track 17. Now try the same action to the slower beat on the CD.

👤 Can half the class do one speed and the other half, the other, at the same time?

Playing percussion at two different speeds at the same time

👤 Transfer the chopping activity above to playing, e.g. woodblocks and claves in two groups at the same time to show the two different speeds of beat.

Rocking to the beat

👤 Grandma rocked backwards and forwards in her rocking chair at the end of the chapter. We are going to rock from side to side. All hold a cuddly toy or doll and sing 'Rock-a-bye Baby' to the nursery rhyme tune with these slightly kinder words!

Rock a bye baby lovely and snug
Rock a bye baby safe in my hug
Rock a bye baby don't make a peep
Rock a bye baby falling a sleep.

Numeracy

Choose seven children to represent Mr Troll, the three little pigs, Hansel, Gretel and Rumplestiltskin. Ask different combinations of characters to group themselves together and make sums accordingly, e.g. Mr Troll and Rumplestiltskin might make a pair, whilst the three little pigs, and Hansel and Gretel might form the other group. Ask the children how many children there are in each group. Put the two groups together and count them all.

Chapter 5
The Gingerbread Man

"You're very brave, Mr Troll!" said the third little pig. "That's two wolves you've scared away."

Mr Troll's cheeks immediately turned pink with embarrassment. "Thank you," he said quietly.

A little further on there came the sudden clatter of racing footsteps. Someone was running very hard and ran right into Mr Troll's leg.

"Steady on!" Mr Troll said. "What's the hurry?"

A tiny gingerbread man was looking up at him fearfully. "Sorry, sorry, sorry! I didn't mean to bash into you. I'm running away from a man and a woman and a cow and a horse. I've got to keep running because they're all after me. They're going to eat me." And with that the gingerbread man rushed off again.

"It's all right," said Mr Troll. "We won't let them catch you."

But the gingerbread man didn't hear. He was already far away, crying, "Run, run as fast as you can. You can't catch me, I'm the gingerbread man!"

"Come on!" said Mr Troll to Hansel and Gretel, Rumplestiltskin and the three little pigs. "Let's try to catch up with him before the man and the woman and the cow and the horse do."

So off they all went. "Run, run, as fast as we can. We've got to catch up with the gingerbread man!" And it wasn't long before they did.

"It's all right," Mr Troll said to the gingerbread man. "You can stop running now!"

"No, no, I can't. They'll catch me and eat me!" replied the gingerbread man, puffing a bit.

"Look, hide inside this hollow tree trunk," said Mr Troll. The gingerbread man did as he was told and presently a man, a woman, a cow and a horse came along.

"Have you seen a gingerbread man?" they asked.

"Yes," said Mr Troll. "He went that way!" Mr Troll pointed towards a cottage where the three bears lived. He knew that for a fact because he'd seen a signpost. So off went the man, the woman, the cow and the horse.

"Oh thank you, Mr Troll. You saved my life," said the gingerbread man when it was safe to come out of the tree trunk. Then he climbed on to Mr Troll's foot and gave him a kiss on his gnarled old leg.

"It was nothing!" said Mr Troll, blushing to the roots of his green hair. "Come and join us, we're looking for somewhere to live."

So off went the party, which was getting fairly big now. Trip trap, trippety trap.

With The Gingerbread Man

CD tracks 18 and 19

1. Jump,   jump,   as   high   as   you   can.___

You   can___   jump___   with   the   gin - ger-bread   man.__

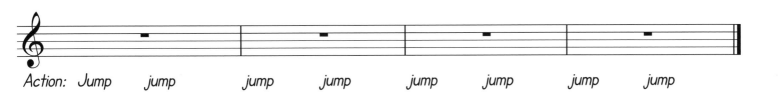

Action: Jump   jump   jump   jump   jump   jump   jump   jump

2. Swim, swim, as strong as you can. You can swim with the gingerbread man.

3. Creep, creep, as quiet as you can. You can creep with the gingerbread man.

4. March, march, as grand as you can. You can march with the gingerbread man.

5. Leap, leap, as far as you can. You can leap with the gingerbread man.

Chapter 5 Activities

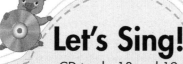

Let's Sing!

CD tracks 18 and 19

🧍 You get out of breath if you try to do movements and singing at the same time so just sing until the music for the actions at the end of each verse, then join in with those actions.

Baking gingerbread men

Ingredients:

330g plain flour

2 level tsp. ground ginger

1 level tsp bicarbonate of soda

120g margarine

180g soft brown sugar

3 tbsp. golden syrup

1 egg

currants

Oven temp: 180 degrees C

Method:

1. Rub flour, marg, ginger and soda together until like breadcrumbs.

2. Mix in sugar, syrup and the egg to make a dough.

3. Roll out and cut into men, put faces and buttons on with the currants.

4. Bake for 15 mins.

More instruments, less instruments

🧍 In the original story of *The Gingerbread Man* the characters chasing the Gingerbread Man accumulate – a woman, a man, a pig, a cow, a horse. Try playing instruments in the same way. Every child has an instrument (doesn't matter what). They should sit in a semicircle and all look at you. Just the child on the end plays at first – you can play to a definite beat or just play. After a few seconds point to the next child, who should join in. Then point to the next child, who also joins in, and continue like this until all the children are playing.

🧍 Talk about that. Did the children notice that the music got louder and louder as each child joined in. But were you able to hear all the sounds? The children should have noticed that some instruments are louder than others and some children play more loudly than others.

🧍 Arrange the instruments so that the quietest one will go first and the loudest last. In this way you will be able to hear each instrument when it first starts playing.

🧍 Now try this activity the other way round, so all the children play together at first. They must really watch you carefully so that when you point to one child at a time, that child will stop playing until only one child is playing and then it is completely silent.

🧍 Talk about this. Were any children late stopping? Children will find this much more challenging than the other way round.

🧍 Try the two activities without a pause between them so you experience the crescendo (growing louder) followed by the decrescendo (growing quieter).

Making up stories and dramatising them

🍪 Read the traditional tale of *The Gingerbread Man* and notice how the story has been adapted to fit 'our' story. The traditional tale is interrupted fairly near the start and continues in a completely different vein with the troll's appearance.

🍪 So stories can go in any direction you want. Introduce the word 'author'.

🍪 Now the children are going to be authors. Make up a very simple story and act it out as you tell it, e.g.

1. **Tom was carefully building a castle with his Duplo one day.**
2. **His cat, Cookie, decided to come and take a look.**
3. **Cookie walked carefully through the Duplo then went to have a sleep.**
4. **His dog, Dibs, decided to take a look. He came bounding over and knocked the castle over.**
5. **Tom was very cross with Dibs.**

🍪 Ask the children to help you recap the story – what happened first? What happened next?

🍪 Now ask them for ideas about how to change it. Guide them along. Ask how you could change the character of the cat? What about changing the character of the dog? What if Tom was doing something completely different in the first place? What if both animals were well behaved? Does Tom finish the castle? Is his mummy happy? Does she give him a special treat? What is it?

Numeracy

How many characters are involved in the story now? Try the activity as at the end of Chapter 4, making sums with eight characters in all.

Moving and observing

🍪 Listen to the song on the CD (track 18) and notice the strong beat of the music. Practise doing the various movements on that beat without any singing this time.

🍪 Now divide the children into five groups – one for each verse. They should take turns doing their allocated movement whilst the others watch and observe whether they are moving precisely on the beat. (Pause the CD in between verses for this.)

🍪 Go for a performance, i.e. play the CD straight through without any pauses.

35

Chapter 6
The Prince

Soon the party came upon the most enormous hedge you have ever seen. It was very thick, very tall and very, very tangly and thorny. A handsome prince was staring at it, shaking his head slowly.

"What's the problem?" Mr Troll asked the prince.

"The problem is that I'm determined to get through this thick hedge because behind it lies a palace. And inside the palace is a princess who has been asleep for a hundred years. I want to wake her with a kiss but how can I possibly get through this hedge? All the branches have spun and woven themselves together."

"This is a job for Rumplestiltskin," said Mr Troll. "Come on, Rumple," he said to the little gnome, "we know you're good at spinning and weaving, but can you undo weaving?"

Rumplestiltskin frowned. "I could try," he said, touching the hedge. And at that very moment something amazing happened. The branches magically started untwining themselves and the hedge opened up leaving a lovely wide pathway straight through to the palace. Rumplestiltskin beamed from ear to ear. "I think my magic might have come back!"

"Oh my! That is magnificent!" exclaimed Mr Troll. Then he turned to the prince. "Well, good luck waking up the princess!" And with that he started to walk off, followed by Rumplestiltskin, the three pigs, Hansel and Gretel and the gingerbread man.

"You can't just go!" said the prince. "I could never have done this without you.
Come and meet the princess."

Mr Troll found himself blushing again as he beamed at the prince.
"Well, if you're sure…"

"Sure I'm sure!" said the prince.

So the happy band followed the prince to the palace. Trip trap, trippety trap.

There Was A Princess Long Ago

CD tracks 20 and 21

A⁹   D   A⁷   D

1. There was a prin-cess long a - go, long a - go, long a - go. There

A⁹   D   A⁷   D

was a prin - cess long a - go. Long a - go.

2. And she lived in a big high tower...

3. A wicked fairy cast a spell...

4. The princess slept for a hundred years...

5. A handsome prince came riding by...

6. He cut the hedge down with his sword...

7. He woke the princess with a kiss...

8. And all the happy people danced...

Chapter 6 Activities

Read the traditional tale - Sleeping Beauty

'Our' story slots in towards the end of the traditional story.

In this chapter we find that Rumplestiltskin has got his magic back and is able to make the hedge part all on its own so let's play some magic games to celebrate.

Let's Sing!
CD tracks 20 and 21

This is a lovely traditional song to sing with small actions while sitting down.

Then find a space of your own and stand up.

Verses 1–4 – remain in your spot whilst singing and doing the action

Verse 5 – gallop round

Verse 6 – stand still whilst singing and doing a big chopping action

Verse 7 – remain in your spot and just do one kiss on your hand and blow it then no more throughout the verse.

Verse 8 – find a partner and dance in ballroom hold(!) or just hold hands and skip round.

The magic solo

For this activity you will need a magic wand.

Everyone sits in a circle.

All the children have an instrument. All play together. This thickly textured sound represents the thick texture of the hedge with its branches all knotted together. If you touch a child lightly on the head with your magic wand, the other children must instantly stop playing so you can just hear one solo sound. This represents the hedge magically unweaving and making a nice pathway through the middle. Have another wand gesture for all the children to resume playing together, then pick another child for the solo. Continue like this.

Magic characters

🧍 You'll need enough cards for the children to have one each with a picture of a pig, or a gnome, or a troll.

🧍 Show the children the three cards you used in 'Pass the Cards' in Chapter 3 and remind them that the troll represented a slow beat, the pig, medium, the gnome, fast.

🧍 The children sit in spaces. Give every child a card with a picture of a troll or a pig or a gnome. They look at their card and make the connection between the character on the card and the relevant speed. Then put the cards face down on the floor.

🧍 You play a drum. If you play a medium beat, all those children who think they've got a medium speed card, i.e. a card with a pig on it, must stand up and join in clapping with the drum beat. When the drum stops they pick up their cards, keeping them hidden, and all go to a random place in the hall allocated by you. Repeat with the other two speeds and send these two groups of children off to two other random places in the hall.

🧍 At this point the children show their cards and you see if the cards have magically grouped themselves together without anyone seeing them or telling anyone else what their card was.

Numeracy
Do the usual sums with the nine characters we have now amassed in the story!

PE and brain gym – Weaving in and out
Place six or seven beanbags or something larger at intervals in a long straight line. The children must take turns weaving (slalom fashion) in and out of the beanbags.

Try the same thing with a 'snake' of children one directly after the other.

Now have just three beanbags at wide intervals. Children take turns to 'draw' a figure of eight on the floor.

Try the same exercise with a 'strong' leader, leading a snake of children round the figure of eight.

Try without the beanbags!

Chapter 7
The Palace

In the gardens and the stables, in the kitchens and the great golden hall, in fact everywhere you looked were servants. But because they'd all fallen asleep right in the middle of doing something or other, they all looked like statues. It was an amazing sight.

The prince led the way up the grand staircase and everyone "oohed" and "aahed" at the sight of the beautiful princess who had been asleep for a hundred years.

"I do hope this works," said the prince.

And with those words he bent down and kissed the princess on the forehead. Instantly she woke up. Then a second later the whole palace was awake too and all the servants were moving about again just as though no time had passed. The princess was so happy to have found her prince at last and insisted that his new friends must live in the palace too. She was enchanted by Rumplestiltskin and said that now his magic had come back he could do magic for her, and if it went away again, not to worry, he could weave her a beautiful carpet. She thought the pigs would make lovely pets and could eat up all the leftover food from the kitchens. "So much better than throwing it away," declared the princess, clapping her hands delightedly. "In fact just as good as recycling!" Then she looked fondly at Hansel and Gretel. "It will be lovely to have some children around the palace," she told them with a smile, and added, "We'll need to get you some toys to play with but at least you've got the gingerbread man as a playmate. In fact any children who come to the palace can play with him too!"

Mr Troll was starting to feel a bit anxious. The princess wanted everyone else to stay but why would she want him? What possible use was an ugly old troll? He started to slip away hoping no one would notice. But he'd only taken a few steps when everyone cried out, "Come back Mr Troll!" Then the first little pig told the prince and princess how Mr Troll had saved all their lives and was the kindest person you could ever meet.

"Mr Troll, I was saving the most important person till last," said the princess, patting his arm. "I was going to ask you if you would be the palace's lucky mascot, but now I know how clever and generous you are, I would like you to also be our chief adviser, and live with us here at the palace for ever!"

Mr Troll could not believe his ears. "That really is too kind, your highness."

"Not at all, not at all," smiled the princess. "And now," she went on excitedly, let's go and have a great big party to celebrate! I'll lead the way."

So off they all went. Trip trap, trippety trap, clip clap, clippety clap, hip hap, hippety hap, hippety hap HOORAY!

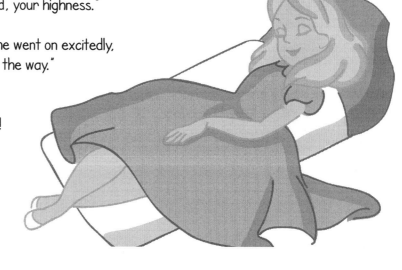

The Princess Pricked Her Finger And...!

CD tracks 22 and 23

1. The king was get - ting dressed,__ the king was get - ting dressed,__ The

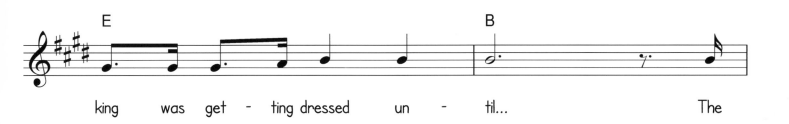

king was get - ting dressed un - til... The

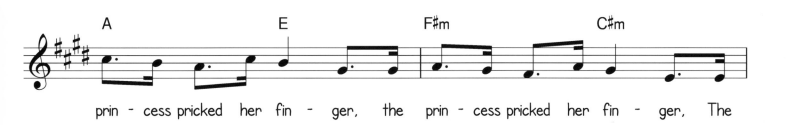

prin - cess pricked her fin - ger, the prin - cess pricked her fin - ger, The

prin - cess pricked her fin - ger and the king... stood still!

2. The queen was eating grapes...

3. The cook was baking cakes...

4. The maid was cleaning floors...

5. The boy was washing up...

6. The groom was rubbing horses...

7. The guard was marching round...

Let's Sing!

Sit and sing the song without actions.

Practise doing appropriate actions for each verse, and stopping like a statue on the word 'still'.

Try a performance of the song, first with everyone doing all the verses and then in seven groups. If it is not your turn to be involved with the actions, you should still sing.

Were the children watching each other doing the actions and stopping? Did everyone stop at exactly the right moment on the word 'still'?

Exploring the palace in drama

Imagine you are exploring the palace. You have been told to stay in your room, but you have sneaked out. The palace is huge and very grand with many staircases and corridors. Walk on tiptoe, slowly, looking to left and right and occasionally look behind you to check no one has seen you. Use CD track 24 as background music for this. Listen carefully for the 'ssh!' sounds in the music. Whenever you hear one, freeze in a very thin shape or a very small shape as though you can hear someone coming and you are hiding. Try to think of a different shape to hide in each time. You might like to practise a few beforehand. There are some wonderful sound effects in this piece. Listen out for the cuckoo clock, the heavy footsteps and the person talking in an echoey voice. The next time you do this activity you might notice even more effects!

The waltz

At the grand party everyone is dancing the waltz. Find a partner and dance freely to the music on CD track 25.

Learn the name 'waltz' in association with dance music in 3-time. Try saying 1,2,3, 1,2,3 etc with the waltz music on the CD. As you say the numbers, clap on number 1 only.

Think of other actions that you could do on the first of the three beats each time, e.g. patting your knees, doing a guitar strum, nodding your head, tapping your toes, 'clapping' the ground. If you really want a challenge, try clapping hands with a partner!

Make a class book

Can you make a simple class picture book out of the story *Mr Troll in Pixiewood Forest*? Or take any character out of the story and create a whole new story for that creature or person.

Art and craft

Make a class 'picture' of the story *Mr Troll in Pixiewood Forest* for the classroom. Choose a particular scene or maybe just show all the characters.

Miming the jobs at the palace

♟ Try out mimes for all the different jobs of the servants in the palace then ask individual children to choose one of the jobs and carry out the action. Can the others guess what the job is?

'In the Hall of the Mountain King'

♟ Play this music on the CD track 26. It is from *Peer Gynt* by Grieg. This story has trolls in it and in this particular music the trolls are all chasing Peer Gynt round the Hall of the Mountain King. They are getting faster and stronger as the music goes on. This might be quite a scary thought for the children, so you might like to 'adapt' this element of the story and say they are playing a game of seeing how quiet they can be at the start, and getting gradually louder, higher and faster. Let the children move freely to the music showing the build-up in whatever way they want.
Warning – this is high-risk stuff!

♟ Each child should have a percussion instrument of their (or your!) choice. Without the CD bring the children in one at a time so the sound accumulates as in the activity 'More instruments, less instruments' in Chapter 5.

♟ Now try this with precision. You will notice that this piece repeats the same phrase of music seventeen times. Arrange the children in ones or twos, according to how many there are in your group, so that you have seventeen lots of one or two. (Children in twos should have the same type of instrument as each other). Bring the children in with a signal or simply by pointing at exactly the right moment with each new phrase. The extension here is that we are emulating the precise structure of the music with the accompanying instruments. Try to play to the beat, although it is not easy as it gets gradually faster. For the last few phrases, all play together.

The character of Mr Troll

Do you think 'our' troll might be one of the trolls in *Peer Gynt*? No. Why not?

Perhaps you can find some troll pictures to show the children.

CD Track Listing

1. Song: Thanks, Mr Troll! (vocal)
2. Song: Thanks, Mr Troll! (backing track)
3. Sad and happy
4. Dramatise the traditional tale of The Three Little Pigs
5. Combining two rhythms
6. Song: The Troll Went Rushing And Racing
7. Poem: The Animals Of The Forest
8. Getting higher and lower
9. Song: Rumplestiltskin Lost His Magic (vocal)
10. Song: Rumplestiltskin Lost His Magic (backing track)
11. Stepping at three different speeds
12. Low and high
13. High, medium and low sounding string instruments
14. High, medium and low sounding woodwind instruments
15. Song: Strolling In The Wood (vocal)
16. Song: Strolling In The Wood (backing track)
17. Chopping wood
18. Song: With The Gingerbread Man (vocal)
19. Song: With The Gingerbread Man (backing track)
20. Song: There Was A Princess Long Ago (vocal)
21. Song: There Was A Princess Long Ago (backing track)
22. Song: The Princess Pricked Her Finger And…! (vocal)
23. Song: The Princess Pricked Her Finger And…! (backing track)
24. Exploring the palace in drama
25. The waltz
26. 'In the Hall of the Mountain King' from *Peer Gynt*

345678